TERRORIZING
THE
NEIGHBORHOOD:

American Foreign Policy

in the

Post-Cold War Era

...many doubtless were enthusiastic about the opportunity to 'kick a little ass' in Panama—

—to borrow some of the rhetoric designed by Bush's handlers as part of their effort to shape an effete New England WASP into a Texas redneck.

Terrorizing the Neighborhood: American Foreign Policy in the Post-Cold War Era

Noam Chomsky

AK Press • Pressure Drop Press
1991

First published in 1991 by:
AK Press, 3 Balmoral Place, Stirling, Scotland, FK8 2RD, UK
Pressure Drop Press, POB 460754, San Francisco, CA 94146, USA

British Library Cataloguing in Publication Data: Chomsky, Noam, 1928— Terrorizing the Neighborhood: American Foreign Policy in the Post-Cold War Era.
1. United States. Foreign relations
 I. Title
327.73

ISBN   1-873176-00-7 (UK)
ISBN   0-9627091-2-3 (USA)

Library of Congress Catalog number: 91-061358
Pressure Drop Press 004

"Arguably the most important intellectual alive, how can he write such nonsense about international affairs and foreign policy?"

-New York Times

This essay is based on a lecture delivered by Noam Chomsky in January 1990 at Edinburgh University, shortly after the U.S. invasion of Panama. It has been rewritten by author, with the addition of footnotes and sources. The lecture was followed by a session of questions and answers, reproduced here as they occured, with editing solely for reasons of style.

This book would not be possible without the assistance of Freddie Baer, Rory Cox, Carol Saunders, Scottish Education and Action for Development (SEAD), Joel Wing, Mat Wright, John Yates, and Tim Yohannan.

The withdrawal of the limited Soviet deter

rent frees the United States to be more

unconstrained in the exercise of violence

Washinton thus has 'more clout.'

Contents

For the United States, the Cold War has been a history of world-wide subversion, aggression and state-run international terrorism, with examples too numerous to mention.

Preface

I was once asked to review *The Chomsky Reader,* a selection of writings by probably the most famous, or—depending on your politics—infamous, Western philosopher of this present era.

Some years earlier I had read some of Chomsky's basic work on linguistics and if I had any criticism of *The Chomsky Reader,* it was the absence in it of that side of his writings. As well as referring to the 'absence' my intention was to indicate some of what 'that side of his writings' might amount to, given that I was doing the review for a general readership.

I then had a hunch there might be a way into it that could at the same time reveal those technical areas which are normally sealed off to the 'general readership.' The review soon became a sort of exploration, an essay.

The importance of Noam Chomsky's contribution to the field of linguistics and the study of mind cannot be overestimated (at the risk of embarrassing the man, one reviewer recently compared his impact to that of Galileo). So what I was intending to do could be dismissed quite reasonably as a piece of presumption, especially by those who believe that 'technical matters' should be left to the 'expert,' the highly skilled and trained 'professional.' But the role of the ordinary person as watchdog on society's 'experts' is crucial to Professor Chomsky's political writings. In general terms, if his work is about any one thing, it is about the primacy of the individual, the essential and fundamental common sense of each and every human being, the facility that allows us to think and judge for ourselves.

The way our education system operates, we are taught

to look at the world as a series of boxes; inside each one is an area of study. The teacher opens certain boxes, never more than one at a time, and lets you peek in. When you finish school the boxes are locked up and the keys all vanish forever.

My own area of specialized knowledge is the writing of prose fiction. Not only am I a 'nonspecialist,' like most people I am a nonspecialist who has great difficulty in tackling subjects like mathematics, computing or logic. In getting to grips with some of the more technical aspects of Chomsky's work I would be dismantling some of the barriers for folk like myself, those who are used to excusing themselves on the grounds of being 'not mechanically-minded.' However, I did have a head start. My introduction to his basic work on linguistics took place during a ten week term at university, where I also studied logic for a spell. The truth is I had no good reason not to embark on the project.

From a different vantage point, every attempt to disseminate technical information for the public at large is an act of political significance. This is why Noam Chomsky's work is so absolutely crucial. Not only is he a major philosopher, he is also a radical thinker of the left who in one way or another has spent most of his life in the struggle against greed. There are at least two things putting him out on the furthest limb:

1. In philosophical terms he is a rationalist. He sets forward what is described as an 'innateness hypothesis.' In academic circles this is usually considered an intellectual anachronism, a throwback most famously to the 17th century French philosopher, Rene Descartes; his position incurs a great deal of hostility from both mainstream right and left.

2. His commitment. He insists on discussing politics at every opportunity, not only in conversation but on the page. He is as likely to publish an article on the secretive and murderous external affairs of his country's government as he is to publish an essay on aspects of transformational

grammar.

His position is ultimately anti-utilitarian and thus in opposition to the J.S. Mill through Bertrand Russell school of Western left-liberalism. Critics from the latter viewpoint occasionally direct attention to the implications of Chomsky's arguments from human nature, that the whole idea of people having fixed (innate) characteristics as individuals is a recipe for an inegalitarian, unequal society and leads to hierarchy. From the right-wing is the dark suspicion (quite justified) that anything smacking of 'the inalienable rights of the individual' must lead to self-determining activity, not only of the sort that ends in 'emancipation' in places like Poland, East Germany and Hungary, but—heaven help us all—in places like Fiji, El Salvador, Kurdistan, Kenya, Angola, Southern Africa, Cambodia, Haiti, Indonesia, Ireland, Italy, Chicago, Birmingham, London, Glasgow, the Indian nations of Canada and so on and so forth.

Not much imagination is required to intuit that links may exist between Western imperialism and the orthodox Western intellectual tradition. Unfortunately there is a massive lack of imagination amongst the mainstream intelligentsia, partly an effect of specialization.

But it is his political activism that sets him beyond the academic pale. Generally, they will hate him for it. By its very nature it instills a shudder at the heart of the intellectual establishment, especially amongst those of his colleagues and peers who place the usual emphasis on such career preoccupations as job security and the accumulation of personal wealth, goods and services.

During my own period at the University of Strathclyde, no time was ever given to Chomsky's political thought; none of his work there appeared on any syllabus. I don't especially hold that against the philosophy section as it then existed; it was a tiny offshoot of the department of English studies and, without an honors course, was deemed worthy of just three full-time lecturers. But I dare say the present generation of students would find that preferable to the current position. In a year or so from now there will be no philosophy course whatsoever at Strathclyde—it is being phased out there as it is elsewhere in the country. How any higher educational establishment lacking a department of philosophy can feel justified in claiming the status of a university is beyond me. It would be an interesting essay topic to set for those in control of our educational system.

Once you leave school, college or university, you are encouraged to stop learning; you are not supposed to find things out; you are taught to leave intellectual matters to those who specialize in them. This goes hand in hand with the fact of existence itself,you are supposed to leave the living of your life to those in control of society's institutions. They won't quite live your life for you (they prefer their own thank you very much) but they will determine how it is to be lived, they'll let you know what's possible and what isn't possible. Our situation is to be like that of children, or of a people or culture under external domination, with the experts as parents or straight colonizers. We are taught to give up the right to determine our own existence.

If Professor Chomsky's philosophical stance is rationalist his politics are libertarian socialist. When I began on the review mentioned at the outset I didn't appreciate the depth of his work, nor the extent of the controversy surrounding it. My own way in involved the heavy application of George Davie's philosophical and historical writings on the generalist, democratic tradition in Scottish education. This tradition is also at sharp odds with the era of the specialist. It is one good reason why the tradition is no longer considered worthy of study. And since it is soundly based in philosophy, it is unusually consistent in that the study of philosophy itself is now being withdrawn from our educational institutions.

Many people coming to Noam Chomsky's essay *American Foreign Policy in the Post-Cold War Era* will be coming to his writings for the first time; a few folk might just be coming to his politics for the first time; more again will be aware of the political but not the linguistic-philosophical dimension. Whatever the position is his work demands a wholehearted exploration. Enjoy it.

James Kelman

(This is an edited version of a talk I did not deliver during the 'Self Determination and Power' event in Glasgow, January 1990, at which Noam Chomsky was the main speaker).

Introduction

In January 1990, Professor Chomsky's reputation as one of America's foremost modern radical thinkers enticed around 500 people to Edinburgh University.

His subject was topical. Central America was in the news again. Panama had just paid a lethal price for its continued presence in Uncle Sam's back yard. Nicaragua was on the brink of electing U.S. favorite Violetta Chamorro to presidential office in a bid to end ten years of U.S.-backed terror and hardship. In El Salvador the U.S.-funded military had reached new depths in its campaign of abduction, torture and murder following the FMLN November uprising. The Cold War may have begun to thaw elsewhere, but in Central America the frosty fingers of U.S. foreign policy continued to squeeze the flesh of the poor, trade unionists, church activists and dissident politicians alike.

Chomsky outlined his damning analysis of American foreign policy which has earned him a place in the rogues' gallery of successive U.S. administrations. He is notorious for his relentless criticisms of U.S. policies, both domestic and foreign. He has exposed his government's proclaimed noble intentions as a facade to conceal essentially right-wing, expansionist designs. Chomsky argues that in the guise of protecting and promoting the ideals of democracy, freedom and justice, the United States is actually sustaining a status quo where the Third World subsidizes U.S. consumption with raw materials and cheap labor. Any attempt by national governments to divert resources for the benefit of the local population, to limit repatriation of profits by U.S. multinationals, or other activities which smack of dangerously independent tendencies are unceremoniously nipped in the bud. The 'communist threat,' until recently invoked whenever the United States resorted to violence against a sovereign state, has proved a convenient smokescreen to justify the indefensible and to rationalize the apparently inexplicable. This singularly unpatriotic analysis is, of course, not helpful to the U.S. establishment, exposing as it does the ultimate goal of both domestic and foreign policy—namely, the perpetuation and enrichment of the powerful elites which own and run the United States. These are the very same groups of individuals and companies which traditionally flex their industrial, economic and military might across much of the globe, undermining elected governments and overriding local interests when necessary.

When, however, the Soviet Union began to dismantle its empire, the communist threat became less credible and U.S. foreign policy-makers were forced to find new enemies. In Panama, President Noriega became distinctly nationalistic just as the Panama Canal was about to pass into Panamanian control. As a result, he underwent a dramatic metamorphosis from CIA-friendly, democratically elected president to anti-democratic, corrupt drug baron in the space of a few editions of the major U.S. dailies. Such new 'threats' to regional stability are therefore not hard to manufacture. So, Chomsky concludes, Central America can look forward to more heavy-handed interference from its powerful northern neighbor.

Central to Chomsky's theory is the observation that self-determination will not be tolerated under any circumstances. This applies not only to Chomsky's analysis of U.S. foreign policy, but also to most political systems in the world today. Almost without exception, nations are governed by small groups which control access to resources, information and power. Chomsky, however, argues that people are quite capable of determining their own lives. He puts faith in the common sense of people to take the most appropriate steps for their own communities. This concept of allowing people to participate in the governance of themselves, reach their own decisions and find their own solutions to problems, is anathema to many mainstream politicians at local and national levels throughout the world. Decentralization and devolution inevitably meet fierce resistance across the political spectrum, with few enlightened exceptions.

One such exception, now under threat, is the experience of the Atlantic Coast of Nicaragua. The Atlantic Coast, with its multi-ethnic population and history of British domination, is very different in character, language and culture from the Spanish-speaking Pacific Coast, and has a long history of separatist movements. When the Sandinistas took power after the revolution in 1979, they attempted to export their policies to the Atlantic Coast with disastrous results. Insensitive to the historical differences and distinct cultural identity of the various local communities, the Sandinista government alienated many of the local Miskito Indians, who formed their own 'contra' forces as a result. A messy situation resulted, exacerbated by government insensitivity on the one hand, and the legacy of the British colonialists on the other, with the Miskitos claiming their historic 'rights' as rulers of the 'Miskito Kingdom'—a British creation of the 18th century. The Sandinistas resolved the problem by taking the unprecedented step of asking the people—individually, door-to-door, in workplaces, in their classrooms—how they thought their region should be run, what powers should rest with the local people and what their relationship should be with the Managua government. Not surprisingly, the answer to these questions was, "I don't know, tell me—how do we go about it?" Such an exercise in Scotland would probably prompt a similar response. Ultimately, however, after a lengthy consultation process involving all the different groups on the Atlantic Coast, the people did develop their own 'Autonomy Process,' reflecting their needs and aspirations.

In the past, development agencies working in the Third World have also been guilty of telling rather than listening, imposing rather than adapting—in short, of assuming that they always knew best. However, many agencies, although they may not know it, are now increasingly accepting Chomsky's analysis by respecting the knowledge, culture and traditional methods of the communities in which they operate. They have begun to recognize that people who may temporarily need support, advice or assistance do not, as a consequence, automatically surrender the right to make decisions for themselves, nor need they abandon their own values and traditions in order to receive assistance. Unfortunately, donor governments and the international financial institutions have yet to be persuaded of this.

SEAD is one of many organizations which supports the fundamental right of people, communities, regions and nations to decide their own future. The problems of achieving this goal, in a world where historically one group's advancement has generally been at the expense of another, cannot be underestimated. The many ethnic conflicts taking place throughout the world today are a direct result of the denial of the right to self-determination which has been going on for decades and, in some cases, centuries. Scotland itself is still seeking recognition of its 'claim of right.'

Chomsky argues that it is the ordinary person—the teacher, the nurse, the mechanic, the factory worker, the bus driver, the peasant—who has the common sense to make the rational decisions upon which the future depends. The governments, international financial institutions and multinational companies which currently wield enormous power on a local and global scale seem incapable of making the fundamental changes necessary to tackle the challenges of poverty and environmental degradation which threaten our very existence. 'Ordinary' people may well find themselves having to pick up the pieces and put them back together using 'common sense.'

Linda Gray
Scottish Education
and Action for Development

The rich and powerful at home have long

appreciated the need to protect themselves

from the destructive forces of free marke

capitalism...

American Foreign Policy in the Post-Cold War Era

When I was invited to speak on Central America a few weeks ago, I thought I would discuss the likely evolution of U.S. policy towards the region in what many see as a post-Cold War era. But before I had a chance to address the question, I was upstaged by the Bush administration, which announced the answer I was intending to give, loud and clear: more of the same.

But not precisely the same. Some adjustments are needed in the propaganda framework. The U.S. invasion of Panama in December is a historic event in one respect. It is the first U.S. act of international violence in the post-World War II era that was not justified by the pretext of a Soviet threat. When the United States invaded Grenada six years earlier, it was still possible to portray the act as a defensive reaction to the machinations of the Russian bear, seeking to strangle us in pursuit of its global designs. John Vessey, Jr., Chairman of the Joint Chiefs of Staff, could intone solemnly that in the event of a Soviet attack on Western Europe, Grenada might interdict the Caribbean sea lanes and prevent the United States from providing oil to its beleaguered allies. Through the 1980s, the attack against Nicaragua was justified by the danger that if we don't stop the Russians there, they'll be pouring across the border at Harlingen, Texas, two days drive away. There are more sophisticated (and equally weighty) variants for the educated classes. But in the case of Panama, not even the imagination of the State Department and the editorial writers extended that far.

Fortunately, the problem had been foreseen. When the White House decided a few years ago that its friend Noriega was getting too big for his britches and had to go, the media took their cue and launched a campaign to convert Noriega, who remained a minor thug exactly as when he was on the CIA payroll, into the most nefarious demon since Attila the Hun. The effort was enhanced by the "war on drugs," a government-media hoax launched a few months earlier in an effort to mobilize the population in fear now that it is becoming impossible to invoke John F. Kennedy's 'monolithic and ruthless conspiracy,' the 'Evil Empire' of Ronald Reagan's speechwriters. It was a smashing success. With a fringe of exceptions after the operation had been completed, the media rallied around the flag with due piety and enthusiasm, funneling the most absurd White House claims to the public while scrupulously refraining from asking the obvious questions, or seeing the most obvious facts.

The Bush administration was, naturally, delighted. A State Department official observed that "the Republican conservatives are happy because we were willing to show some muscle, and the Democratic liberals can't criticize because it's being so widely seen as a success."[1] The State Department followed the standard newspeak conventions in contrasting 'conservatives,' who advocate a powerful and violent state, to 'liberals,' who sometimes disagree with the 'conservatives' on tactical grounds. These salutary developments "can't help but give us more clout," the same official continued.

As for the general population, many doubtless were also enthusiastic about the opportunity to 'kick a little ass' in Panama—to borrow some of the rhetoric designed by George Bush's handlers as part of their comical effort to shape an effete New England WASP into a Texas redneck. But it is interesting to read the letters to the editor in major newspapers, which tend to express hostility to the aggression, along with much shame and distress, and often provide analysis

1. Stephen Kurkjian and Adam Pertman, *Boston Globe*, January 5, 1990.

and insights that the professionals have been careful to avoid. A not untypical professional reaction was given by the respected *Washington Post* correspondent David Broder. He notes that there has been some carping at "the prudence of Bush's action" from "the left" (meaning, some centrist liberals, anything else being far beyond his horizons, as is the idea that there might be criticism on grounds other than prudence). But he dismisses "this static on the left" with scorn: "what nonsense." Rather, the invasion of Panama helped clarify the "new national consensus" on "the circumstances in which military intervention makes sense." The "best single definition" of the new consensus was given by Reagan's defense secretary, Caspar Weinberger, who outlined six criteria which are "well-considered and well-phrased." Four of them state that intervention should be designed to succeed. The other two add that the action should be "vital to our national interest" and a "last resort" to achieve it.[2] Oddly, Broder neglected to add the obvious remark about these impressive criteria: they could readily have been invoked by Hitler.

Continuing to explore the consensus, Broder believes that "Democratic nominee Michael Dukakis, after floundering around on the question of military interventions, came up with a set of standards strikingly similar to Weinberger's" during the 1988 presidential campaign. These standards, as outlined by his senior foreign policy adviser, were that U.S. force could be used "to deter aggression against its territory, to protect American citizens, to honor our treaty obligations and take action against terrorists" after peaceful means had failed. "The Panama invasion met all of those tests," Broder concluded. One can appreciate the joyful mood among State Department propagandists. Even they did not dare to claim to be deterring Panamanian aggression or taking action against terrorists. And while

2. Broder, 'When U.S. Intervention Makes Sense,' *Washington Post Weekly*, January 22, 1990.

there was the ritual gesture towards international law, it was neither intended seriously nor taken seriously. Even traditional jingoists would go no further than to say that the "legalities are murky" (editors of the *Wall Street Journal*.)[3] In fact, it is transparently impossible to reconcile the invasion with the supreme law of the land, as codified in the U.N. Charter, the Organization of American States (OAS) Treaty, or the Panama Canal Treaty. Hardly less ludicrous is the claim, to which we return, that the invasion aimed to protect American citizens.

Broder is pleased that "we have achieved a good deal of clarity in the nation on this question (of the right of intervention), which divided us so badly during and after the Vietnam War," and this "important achievement...should not be obscured by a few dissident voices on the left," with their qualms about the prudence of the action. Despite the abysmal intellectual and moral level of the performance, Broder may well be right about the consensus. His evaluation recalls a comment by one of the most significant figures in 20th century America, the radical pacifist A.J. Muste: "The problem after a war is with the victor. He thinks he has just proved that war and violence pay. Who will now teach him a lesson?"

Ever since the latter days of the Indochina wars, elite groups have been concerned over the erosion of popular support for force and subversion—what is termed the 'Vietnam syndrome.' Intensive efforts have been made to cure the malady, but so far in vain. The Reaganites assumed that it had been overcome by the propaganda triumphs over postwar Indochina, Afghanistan and Iran. They learned differently when they tried to return to the traditional pattern of intervention in Central America, and were forced to retreat to clandestine and indirect measures to terrorize and intimidate popular forces seeking democracy and re-

3. Headline, Frederick Kempe and Jose de Cordoba, *Wall Street Journal*, December 26, 1989.

form. Through the 1980s, hopes have been voiced that we have finally overcome "the sickly inhibitions against the use of military force" (Norman Podhoretz, referring to the glorious triumph in Grenada). In the more nuanced tones of the liberal commentator, Broder, too, is expressing the hope that finally the population has been restored to health and will end its childish obsession with the rule of law and human rights. His "new consensus," however, is largely illusory, restricted to the sectors who have always recognized that the global designs of U.S. power require the freedom to resort to state violence, terror and subversion. The new consensus is more properly described as a heightened self-confidence on the part of those who shared the old consensus.

This renewed self-confidence on the part of proponents of intervention, including liberals of the Broder variety, may well reduce some of the internal constraints on the resort to violence and subversion. But there are conflicting factors that limit these options. It is understood across the spectrum that it would be 'imprudent' to attack anyone capable of fighting back. It's one thing to strike manly poses and exult in heroic exploits after attacking Panama, already under virtual U.S. military occupation; or Grenada, defended by a handful of militia and Cuban construction workers with no military training; or Libya, defenseless against bombardment.[4] But those who revel in the new jingoism are surely aware that the consensus is fragile, and will vanish if violence faces resistance, while much of the population remains infected by the Vietnam syndrome despite all efforts to overcome it. Intervention is still further con-

---

4. See *WSJ*, January 15, 1990 for a recent review of the military fiasco in Grenada; on the role of the media in suppressing the crucial facts about the invasion, see my *Necessary Illusions* (South End, 1989). On the government-media fraud concerning the Libya bombardment, see my *Pirates and Emperors* (Claremont, 1986; Amana, Black Rose, Montreal).

strained by the relative decline in U.S. power, accelerated by the economic mismanagement of the Reaganites. The 'new clarity' on the right of forceful intervention is likely to have limited consequences. Let's put Panama aside for the moment and turn to more general questions. Note first that there are several reasons why it makes sense to expect the post-Cold War era to be much like what came before, apart from matters of tactics and propaganda.

The Cold War has regularly been portrayed as a superpower conflict. So it was, but that is only a fraction of the truth. Reality protrudes when we look at the typical events and practices of the Cold War.

On Moscow's side, the Cold War is illustrated by tanks in East Berlin, Budapest, Prague and more recently the invasion of Afghanistan, the one case of Soviet military intervention well outside the historic invasion route from the West. Domestically, the Cold War served to entrench the power of the military-bureaucratic elite whose power derives from the Bolshevik coup of 1917.

For the U.S., the Cold War has primarily been a history of worldwide subversion, aggression and state-run international terrorism, with examples too numerous to mention. Secondarily, it has served to maintain U.S. influence over the industrial allies, and to suppress independent politics and popular activism, an interest shared by local elites. The domestic counterpart within the United States has been to entrench the military-industrial complex that elicited Eisenhower's farewell warning—in essence, a smoothly functioning welfare state for the rich with a national security ideology for population control. The major institutional mechanism is a system of state industrial management to sustain high tech industry, relying on the taxpayer to fund research and development and provide a state-guaranteed market for waste production. This crucial gift to the corporate manager has been the domestic function of the Pentagon system (including NASA and the Department of Energy, which controls nuclear weapons production); benefits ex-

In the post-Vietnam period, elites understood that it would be necessary to take stern measures to restore U.S. power and corporate profits. That required an interventionist policy abroad and a determined class war at home.

tend to the computer and electronics industries and other sectors of the advanced industrial economy. The Cold War has provided a large part of the underpinnings for the system of public subsidy and private profit that is proudly called Free Enterprise.

We may take note of the broad if tacit understanding that the capitalist model has limited application; business leaders have long recognized that it will not do for them. The successful industrial societies depart radically from this model, as has generally been true in the past—one reason why they are successful industrial societies. In the United States, the sectors of the economy that remain competitive internationally are those that feed from the public trough: high tech industry, capital-intensive agriculture, pharmaceuticals and others. The glories of Free Enterprise provide a useful weapon against government policies that might benefit the mass of the population; and of course, capitalism will do just fine for the former colonies—now including, it is hoped, the former Soviet empire as it collapses and is subjected to Western needs. For the regions that are to provide such benefits as cheap labor, resources, markets, tax-free havens and opportunities to export pollution, the model is highly recommended; it facilitates their exploitation. But these doctrines must be restricted to the proper targets. The rich and powerful at home have long appreciated the need to protect themselves from the destructive forces of free market capitalism, which may provide suitable themes for rousing oratory, but only so long as the public handout is secure, the regulatory apparatus is in place and state power is on hand to ensure proper obedience on the part of the lower orders.

Putting it schematically, for the Soviet Union the Cold War has been primarily a war against its satellites; and for the United States a war against the Third World, with ancillary benefits with regard to domination of the other industrial societies. For both superpowers, the Cold War has served to entrench a certain system of domestic privilege and coercion. The policies pursued within the Cold War framework have, naturally, been unattractive to the general population, which accepts them only under duress. Throughout history, the standard device to mobilize a reluctant population has been the fear of an evil enemy, dedicated to our destruction. The superpower conflict served the purpose admirably. The Cold War has had a functional utility for the superpowers, one reason why it has persisted.

These central features of the Cold War system help explain its typical events and practices, and also the ideological constructions that have accompanied it. In the West, it is regularly conceded well after the fact (the fact being some exercise of subversion or aggression in the Third World, or renewed benefits through the Pentagon system at home) that the threat of Soviet aggression was exaggerated, the problems misconstrued and the idealism that guided the actions misplaced. But the requisite beliefs remain prominently displayed on the shelf. However fanciful, they can be served up to the public when needed—often with perfect sincerity, in accord with the familiar process by which useful beliefs arise from perceived interests.

Recent history provides many examples. In the post-Vietnam period, elites understood that it would be necessary to take stern measures to restore U.S. power and corporate profits. That required an interventionist policy abroad and a determined class war at home. As a virtual reflex, the policies were justified by rampaging Soviet power. In fact, as the CIA now quietly concedes, Soviet military spending, which had surged after the dramatic demonstration of Soviet weakness during the Cuban missile crisis, began to level off in the mid-1970s, exactly the opposite of what was claimed in the West in order to justify the Carter-Reagan military buildup and attack on social programs.

The breakup of the Portuguese empire and the failure of the U.S. effort to maintain Western control over Indochina were interpreted as evidence that the Soviet Union was marching on from strength to strength, even establishing its domination of such international powerhouses as Grenada, South Yemen and Nicaragua. The fact of the matter is that Soviet power worldwide had been declining since its peak (which was not very high, in comparison to the United States) since about 1960. More generally, both superpowers had been declining in their power to coerce and control since about that time—a relative decline, of course; in absolute terms, the power to destroy always advances.

But no matter how exotic the claims and the intellectual constructions, it was always fair to assume that they would be taken seriously by the docile intelligentsia. The more critical might say, as usual, that the threat was exaggerated, but the basic assumptions of the propaganda framework were very rarely challenged. The services of the left should, incidentally, not be underestimated. Now one side has called off the game, at least temporarily. It is not true that the Cold War has ended. Rather, it has perhaps half-ended. For the United States, which remains a player as before, the change in the rules requires new forms of propaganda and some tactical adjustments—a problem. But there is a compensating gain. The withdrawal of the limited Soviet deterrent frees the United States to be more unconstrained in the exercise of violence. Washington thus has 'more clout.' Recognition of these welcome possibilities has been explicit in public discourse from the early stages of Soviet initiatives towards *detente,* as I have discussed elsewhere. Expressing his pleasure over the invasion of Panama, Elliott Abrams observed that "Bush probably is going to be increasingly willing to use force." The use of force is more feasible than before, he explained, now that "developments in Moscow have lessened the prospect for a small operation to escalate into a superpower conflict."[5]

Similarly, the test of Gorbachev's 'New Thinking' is

5. Kurkjian and Pertman, *op. cit.;* latter quote is the interviewer's paraphrase.

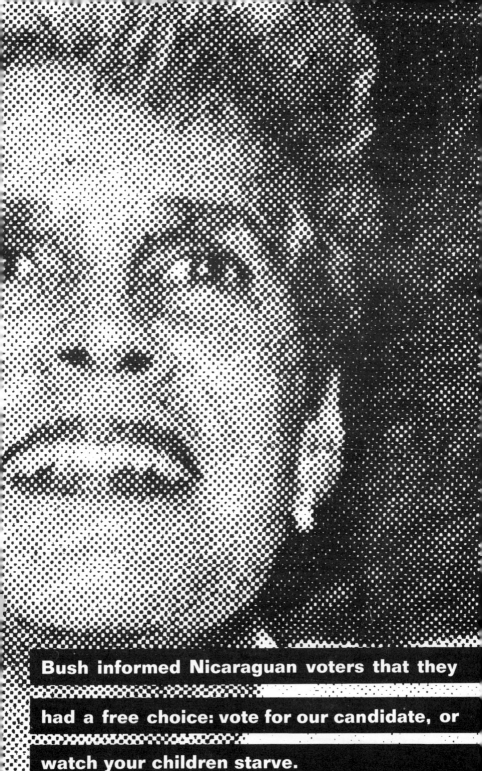

Bush informed Nicaraguan voters that they had a free choice: vote for our candidate, or watch your children starve.

regularly taken to be his willingness to withdraw support from those whom the United States is trying to destroy; only if he allows us to have our way will we know that he is serious about *detente*. This interpretation is entirely natural in a lawless, terrorist political culture, and therefore elicits little comment or even notice.

Notice that the Russian moves have helped to dispel some conventional mystification. The official story has always been that we contain the Russians, deterring them and thwarting their global designs. But the reality, as has been evident from the start, is that the fear of potential superpower conflict has repeatedly served to contain and deter the United States. What is termed 'Soviet aggression' in the Third World has typically consisted of moves by the Kremlin to protect and sustain targets of U.S. attack. Now that the Soviet Union is limiting, perhaps terminating, these efforts, the United States is freer to pursue its global designs by force and violence, and the rhetorical clouds begin to lift.

To summarize, one reason to expect that U.S. policy towards Central America will be 'more of the same' after the Cold War has ended is that the crucial event hasn't taken place. As I said earlier, viewed realistically, the Cold War has at most half-ended. Its apparent termination is an ideological construction more than a historical fact, based on an interpretation that masks some of its essential functions. For the United States, much of the basic framework of the Cold War remains intact, apart from the modalities of population control. The latter problem—a central problem facing any state or other system of power—still remains, and will have to be addressed in new and more imaginative ways as traditional Cold War doctrine loses its efficacy.

There is also a deeper reason why U.S. policy in Central America, and elsewhere, is likely to pursue essentially the same course as before, with adjustments in tactics and propaganda. Within a narrow range of variation, policies express institutional needs. U.S. policies have been stable over a long period because the dominant institutions are stable, and subject to very little internal challenge. Politics and ideology are largely bounded by the consensus of the business community. On critical issues, there is tactical debate within the mainstream, but questions of principle rarely arise. To recall a striking case, during the Indochina wars and since, the framework of 'defense of South Vietnam' was unchallenged among the political elites and educated classes. They could easily perceive that the Soviet Union invaded Afghanistan and that the pretense to be defending it was an absurdity, but claims of similar character and validity by the U.S. propaganda system passed without challenge. The trivial fact that the United States had invaded South Vietnam and virtually destroyed it was unthinkable, and remains so.

Extraordinary historical circumstances have also safeguarded U.S. institutions from any serious external challenge. After World War II, the United States was in a position of relative power, wealth and security without historical parallel. The conventional description of the Cold War system as bipolar is rather misleading; the Soviet Union was always a junior partner in world management and was never even close to being an economic rival. Other challenges to U.S. dominance have arisen over the years; these have influenced tactical decisions, and may do so significantly as they continue to mount.

The basis of policy is outlined with considerable clarity in the internal record of planning during and after World War II.[6] The Third World is to 'fulfill its main function as a source of raw materials and a market' for the industrial societies, which were to be reconstituted within a global order subordinated to the needs of the United States (meaning: dominant elites within it). In Latin America, as elsewhere, "the protection of our resources" must be a major

---

6. For details and references, see my *Turning the Tide* (1985), *On Power and Ideology* (1987). Also Gabriel Kolko, *Confronting the Third World* (Pantheon, 1988).

concern, the influential State Department planner George Kennan explained. Since the main threat to 'our resources,' and our interests generally, is indigenous, we must realize, Kennan continued, that "the final answer might be an unpleasant one," namely "police repression by the local government.""Harsh government measures of repression" should cause us no qualms as long as "the results are on balance favorable to our purposes." In general, "it is better to have a strong regime in power than a liberal government if it is indulgent and relaxed and penetrated by Communists." The term 'Communist' is used here in the technical sense it has assumed in American political discourse, referring to labor leaders, peasant organizers, priests organizing self-help groups, and anyone who has the wrong priorities and thus gets in our way.

The right priorities are explained in the highest level top secret documents. The major threats to U.S. interests are persistently identified as 'nationalist regimes' that are responsive to popular pressures for "immediate improvement in the low living standards of the masses" and diversification of the economies for domestic needs. This dangerous tendency conflicts not only with the need to "protect our resources," but also our concern to encourage "a climate conducive to private investment" and "in the case of foreign capital to repatriate a reasonable return." The Kennedy administration identified the roots of U.S. interest in Latin America as in part military (the Panama Canal, strategic raw materials, etc.), but perhaps still more "the economic root whose central fiber is the $9 billion of private U.S. investment in the area" and extensive trade relations. The need "to protect and promote American investment and trade" is threatened by nationalism, sometimes called 'ultranationalism'; that is, efforts to follow an independent course, interfering with the functions that the region is to fulfill. The preference is for agro-export models serving the interests of U.S.-based agribusiness, chemical and energy corporations (pesticides and fertilizers, in particular), and

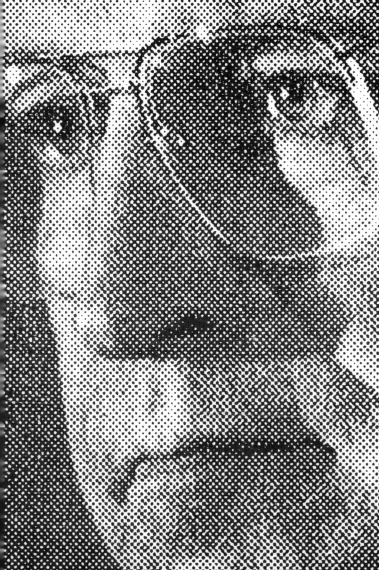

..it's not that U.S. policy-makers like torture.

Rather, it is an irrelevance.

in later years, cheap labor for assembly plants, unsupervised banking and other useful services.

These policies, too, tend to be unpopular in the targeted countries, but for their populations, no subtle measures of control are necessary. Under an Agency for International Development (AID) cover, 'public safety missions' trained local police forces. The principle, as outlined by the State Department, was that the police "first detect discontent among people" and "should serve as one of the major means by which the government assures itself of acceptance by the majority." An effective police force can often abort unwanted developments that might otherwise require "major surgery" to "redress these threats" with "considerable force." But police violence may not suffice. Accordingly, U.S. planners stressed the need to gain control over the Latin American military, described as "the least anti-American of any political group." Converting the mission of the military from 'hemispheric defense' to 'internal security,' the Kennedy liberals and their successors were able to overcome the problem of 'ultranationalism' by establishing and backing National Security States on a neo-Nazi model, with consequences that are well-known. These measures also overcame the concerns expressed in the internal record over the excessive liberalism of the Latin American govemrnents, the protection of rights afforded by their legal systems, and the completely unacceptable free flow of ideas, which undercut U.S. efforts at indoctrination and ideological control. Where the police and military cannot be controlled directly, as in post-Somoza Nicaragua or Panama, it is necessary to overthrow the government and install a more compliant regime.

These policies are givens; they are subject to no challenge and no debate. It would be misleading to say that there is near unanimity on these matters in Congress, the media and the intellectual community. More accurately, the basic doctrines are out of sight, out of mind, like the air we breathe, beyond the possibility of recognition, let alone discussion. Within the framework established by these invariant principles, debate is legitimate, indeed encouraged; not only because there are tactical differences among elites that should be aired and clarified for their benefit, but also because lively controversy (crucially, within proper bounds) provides the sense that the formal freedoms actually function, an essential means of population control when appeal to force is not a viable option.

These invariant conditions have certain consequences. One is the striking correlation between U.S. aid and human rights abuses. Lars Schoultz, the leading U.S. academic specialist on human rights and U.S. foreign policy in Latin America, found that U.S. aid "has tended to flow disproportionately to Latin American governments which torture their citizens...to the hemisphere's relatively egregious violators of fundamental human rights." The correlation is strong, includes military aid, is unrelated to need, and persists through the Carter human rights administration. Reaganite support for mass slaughter and terror makes it superfluous to raise the question for this grim era. Other studies have found the same phenomenon worldwide. The reason is not that U.S. policy-makers like torture. Rather, it is an irrelevance. What matters is to bar independent development and the wrong priorities, and for this purpose, it is often necessary (regrettably) to murder priests, torture union leaders, 'disappear' peasants, and otherwise intimidate the general population. Governments with the right priorities will therefore be led to adopt such measures. Since the right priorities are associated with U.S. aid, we find the secondary correlation between U.S. aid and human rights violations.

A second consequence is the general U.S. opposition to social reform, unless it can be carried out in conformity to overriding U.S. interests (meaning, again, the interests of the privileged classes). While this is occasionally possible in the Third World, such circumstances are rare. Even where social reform could be pursued along with subordination to

U.S. interests (Costa Rica is the obvious example), Washington has reacted with considerable ambivalence.[7]

A third consequence is the extreme hostility of the U.S. government towards democracy. The reason is obvious: a functioning democracy will be responsive to appeals from the masses of the population and will be likely to succumb to excessive nationalism.

Democratic forms are, of course, acceptable, even praiseworthy, if only for purposes of population control at home. But they are acceptable only when they function within the prescribed bounds. Honduras is a case in point. It's November 1989 elections received scanty but generally favorable coverage in the U.S. media, which described them as "a milestone for the United States, which has used Honduras as evidence that the democratically elected governments it supports in Central America are taking hold."[8]

A closer look shows just how they are taking hold. The November elections were effectively restricted to the two traditional parties. One candidate was from a family of wealthy industrialists, the other from a family of large landowners. Their top advisers "acknowledge that there is little substantive difference between the two and the policies they would follow as president," the press reports.[9] Both parties represent large landowners and industrialists and have close ties with the military, the effective rulers, who are independent of civilian authority under the Honduras Constitution but heavily dependent on the United States, as is the economy. The Guatemalan *Central America*

---

7. See *Necessary Illusions* for a review of the declassified record and other relevant material.
8. Wilson Ring, *Boston Globe, November 24,* 1989. Also *New York Times,* November 24. For further references, here and below, see my manuscript *Tasks Ahead IV: Post-Cold War Cold War,'* published without notes in *Z Magazine* (Boston), March 1990.
9. Ring, *op. cit.*

Report adds that "in the absence of substantial debate, both candidates rely on insults and accusations to entertain the crowds at campaign rallies and political functions." Popular participation was limited to ritual voting. The legal opposition parties (Christian Democratic and Social Democratic) charged massive electoral fraud.

Human rights abuses by the security forces escalated as the election approached. In the weeks before the election, there were attacks with bombs and rifle fire against independent political figures, journalists and union leaders. In preceding months, the armed forces launched a campaign of political violence, including assassination of union leaders and other extrajudicial executions, leaving tortured and mutilated bodies by roadsides for the first time. The human rights organization C.O.D.E.H. reports that at least 78 people were killed by the security forces between January and July, while reported cases of torture and beatings more than tripled over the preceding year. But torture and death squad operations remained at a low enough level so as not to disturb elite opinion.

Starvation and general misery are rampant, the extreme concentration of wealth has increased during the decade of 'democracy,' and 70 percent of the population is malnourished. Despite substantial U.S. aid and no guerrilla threat, the economy is collapsing, with capital flight and a sharp drop in foreign investment, and almost half of export earnings devoted to debt service. All of this, too, is a complete irrelevance for the masters, as long as there is no major threat to order and profits flow.[10]

In short, Honduras is quite an acceptable democracy, and there is no concern over the 'level playing field' for the

10. *Central America Bulletin* (CARIN), August 1989, Council on Hemispheric Affairs, *News and Analysis*, November 24; *Washington Report on the Hemisphere*, November 22; *Central America Report* (Guatemala), November 17, 24; *Latinamerica Press* (Peru) August 24, 1989.

elections, unlike Nicaragua.

Even El Salvador and Guatemala, murderous gangster states run by the U.S.-backed military, are considered democracies—sometimes 'fledgling democracies.' Elite opinion expresses considerable pride in having established and maintained these charnel houses, with 'free elections' permitted after 'the playing field had been levelled' by Pol Pot-style terror, including mass slaughter, torture, disappearance, mutilation and other effective devices. Physical destruction of the independent media and murder of editors and journalists who do not toe the line passed virtually without comment—often literally without report—among their Western colleagues.

Colombia, too, is described as a democracy, though a democracy under threat from narco-traffickers. By congressional and media standards, however, democracy is not under threat because the two parties that share political power are "two horses (with) the same owner" (former President Alfonso Lopez Michaelsen)—rather as in the United States. Nor is 'democratic normalcy' threatened by a system with such features as these: death squads have killed about 1,000 members of the one party not owned by the oligarchy (Union Patriotica) since its founding in 1985, leaving the unions and popular organizations with no meaningful political representation; disappearance and execution of labor, Indian and community leaders is a regular part of daily life while "many Colombians insist that army troops often act as though they were an occupation force in enemy territory" (Americas Watch); these death squads dedicated to extermination of 'subversives' are in league with the security forces (Amnesty International); the death squads sow "an atmosphere of terror, uncertainty and despair," and "all families in which even one member is somehow involved in activities directed towards social justice" are under constant threat of disappearance and torture, conducted with 'impunity' by the military and their allies (Pax Cristi), including 'cocaine gangs' and the owner

What matters is to bar independent develop-

ment and the wrong priorities, and for this

purpose it is often necessary to murder priests,

torture union leaders, 'disappear' peasants,

and otherwise intimidate the general popula-

tion.

of the two horses. All of this leaves the playing field level and poses no threat to 'democratic institutions,' no challenge to "America's historic purpose of advancing the cause of freedom in the world," to quote a leading U.S. scholar.

Occasionally, one hears an honest comment. For example, Joachim Maitre of Boston University, one of the leading academic supporters of Reagan administration policies in Central America, observes candidly that the United States has "installed democracies of the style of Hitler Germany" in El Salvador and Guatemala. But such praiseworthy willingness to face the facts is far from the norm.

Although democracy is acceptable when pursued in the manner of U.S. terror states, strong measures must be taken to prevent it when popular organizations are allowed to function, threatening the monopoly of the political system by the business-landowner elite. Signs of such deviation, as in El Salvador and Guatemala a decade ago, require that the death squads be unleashed to administer a dose of reality and to 'level the playing field' so that 'democracy' can be restored. Similarly, alarm bells ring when a government comes to power "that cares for its people," in the words of Jose Figueres, the founder of Costa Rican democracy, referring to the Sandinistas, who brought Nicaragua the first such government in its history and should be allowed "to finish what they started in peace; they deserve it." For expressing such improper sentiments, this leading figure of Central American democracy has been censored from the free press in the United States.[11]

Such transgressions plainly require stern discipline. Accordingly, hostility to the Sandinistas has been uniform in elite circles. This is no exaggeration. Surveys of opinion pieces in the national press at peak periods of debate over policy towards Nicaragua reveal close to 100 percent conformity to this requirement—that is, conformity at the level of

11. See *Necessary Illusions* and sources cited there.

a well-run totalitarian state. No less interesting are the topics excluded from discussion. There is no mention of the fact that unlike the U.S. clients, the Sandinistas, whatever their sins, did not slaughter their own populations. The equally uncontroversial fact that they attempted social reforms and directed resources to the needs of the poor majority receives passing mention in about two percent of commentary surveyed. The figures reflect the significance accorded to mass slaughter and the suffering of the poor within U.S. political culture, relative to more important matters that guide policy.

The media included tactical debate over the best way to restore Nicaragua to 'the Central American mode' and impose 'regional standards'—those of the U.S. client states. That fact is often put forth as proof of the independence and even adversarial nature of the media. But it is hardly surprising, given that by 1986 some 80 percent of leadership elements (corporation executives, etc.) were opposed to the contra option, recognizing that there are more cost-effective ways to strangle and destroy a weak and small country completely dependent on its relations with the U.S. for survival. Even if the media were solely serving as a propaganda instrument for the nexus of state-private power, they would permit, indeed encourage, such discussion.

In Congress as well, debate kept to the question of how best to rid ourselves of the Sandinistas. Should we use violence and terror, as the Reaganites demanded? Or should we find other ways to ensure that the government "festers in its own juices," as the leading Democratic dove senator, Alan Cranston, preferred: embargo, blocking foreign aid, etc. As distinct from Honduras and the two outright terror states where everything is in order, Nicaraguan elections are a matter of deep concern, and from the outset of the electoral campaign the U.S. interfered massively to gain victory for its candidates. Some attention has been given to the enormous financial aid to the U.S.-backed candidates, amounting to about half the combined monthly wage of every person in Nicaragua. But this is the least part of the effort to undermine free elections. Far more significant, and considered quite uncontroversial, are such actions as the White House statement of November 1989 promising "to lift the trade embargo and assist in Nicaragua's reconstruction" if the U.S. candidate, Violeta Chamorro, wins the election, issued as she opened her campaign at a meeting in Washington with President Bush. In brief, Bush informed Nicaraguan voters that they had a free choice: vote for our candidate, or watch your children starve. In such ways we 'level the playing field.' For deeply committed totalitarians, elections conducted under such conditions are 'free and fair.'

A second and perhaps still more extreme form of U.S. intervention to bar the threat of free elections, considered not only uncontroversial but meritorious, was the 'peace process' scam conducted with the cooperation of Costa Rican president Oscar Arias since 1987. Here the record is very clear, though brilliantly concealed by the loyal media in the United States and Europe. A series of agreements were made, each intended by the United States and its clients to be observed by Nicaragua but to be violated by every other participant. Each successive step left the U.S. allies free to pursue their programs of violence and repression, and maintained the contra threat in violation of the agreements, while Nicaragua was subjected to microscopic examination. Any minor deviation from the increasingly narrow strictures led to impassioned denunciation by Arias and other cynics, who remained silent, or even approved (as in the case of Arias) when the U.S. clients carried out far worse abuses. This was a highly successful procedure, continued right through the electoral campaign, to ensure that the U.S. candidate would be able to offer a credible promise that the contra terror would be ended, while the Sandinistas could offer only more suffering. The U.S.-Arias diplomacy is a perfect example of Stalinist-style 'salami tactics,' regarded as quite praiseworthy by Western opinion.

...National Public Radio amused its elite intel-

ectual audience with an interview with a fruit

nd vegetable dealer who was asked whether

Noriega's pock-marked face really did look

ke a pineapple.

We learn a good deal about Western culture, and its profound contempt for democracy, by observing this charade over the past several years.[12]

In this context, we may return briefly to the Panama invasion. After offering a series of pretexts, the White House settled on the need to "protect American lives." The White House announced that there had been "literally hundreds of cases of harassment and abuse of Americans" in recent months by Noriega's forces—though, curiously, they issued no warning to Americans to stay away, up until the day of the invasion. A U.S. soldier was killed under disputed circumstances, but what tipped the scales was the threat to the wife of an officer who was arrested and beaten. Bush "often has difficulty in emotionally charged situations," the *New York Times* reported, "but his deep feelings clearly came through" when he spoke of this incident, proclaiming in his best Ollie North rendition that "this president" is not going to stand by while American womanhood is threatened.[13] The press did not explain why "this president" refused even to issue a protest when a few weeks earlier an American nun, Diana Ortiz, had been kidnapped, tortured, and sexually abused by the Guatemalan police—or why the media did not find the story worth reporting when it appeared on the wires on November 6, and have ignored repeated calls for an investigation by religious leaders and Congressional representatives. Nor were Bush's "deep feelings" contrasted with the response of "this president" to the treatment of American women and other religious and humanitarian workers in El Salvador a few weeks later, a small footnote to the brutal government actions praised by Secretary of State James Baker at a November 29 press conference as "absolutely appropriate"—a comment that

---

12. For extensive details, see *Necessary Illusions*
13. Marlin Fitzwater, *Boston Globe*, December 20, 1989; Andrew Rosenthal, *New York Times*, December 22, 1989.

was suppressed, perhaps regarded as not too useful in the midst of the furor about the murder of the Jesuit priests.[14]

Another pretext for the invasion was our commitment to democracy, deeply offended when Noriega stole the 1989 election that had been won by the U.S.-backed candidate, Guillermo Endara, now placed in office by the invasion. An obvious test comes to mind: what happened in the preceding election in 1984, when Noriega was still *our* thug? The answer is that Noriega stole the election with more violence than in 1989, barring the victory of Arnulfo Arias and installing Nicolas Ardito Barletta, since known in Panama as 'fraudito.' Washington opposed Arias, who was considered a dangerous nationalist, preferring Barletta, whose campaign was financed with U.S. government funds through the National Endowment for Democracy, according to U.S. Ambassador Everett Briggs. George Shultz was sent down to legitimatize the fraud, praising "Panamanian democracy" at the inauguration. The media thoughtfully looked the other way.

Our 1989 favorite, Guillermo Endara, was close to Arias and remained his spokesman in Panama until his death in 1988 in self-imposed exile. The *Washington Post* now reports that Endara was chosen to run in 1989 "largely because of his close ties to the late legendary Panamanian politician Arnulfo Arias, who was ousted from the presidency by the military three times since the 1940s"—accurate, but crucially selective. The media once again looked the other way when, during the invasion, Endara denounced the "fraud of 1984," and they do not ask why our fabled 'yearning for democracy' was mysteriously awakened only when Noriega had become a nuisance to Washington

14. Associated Press, November 6, December 2, 1989; January 6 1980. AP, *Miami Herald,* November 7, 1989; Patti McSherry, *In These Times,* December 20, 1989; Baker, Rita Beamish, AP, November 29, 1989.

rather than an asset.[15] Other pretexts were equally weighty, and need not detain us.

The reasons for the invasion were plain enough, but largely avoided in media commentary. As is well-known, Manuel Noriega had been working happily with U.S. intelligence since the 1950s, right through the tenure of George Bush as CIA director and later Drug Czar for the Reagan administration. By the mid-1980s, however, the United States was beginning to reassess his role and decided to remove him. A largely middle and upper class civic opposition developed, leading to street protests that were brutally suppressed by the Panamanian military under the command of Colonel Eduardo Herrera Hassan. Hassan's troops "most energetically shot, gassed, beat and tortured civilian protesters during the wave of demonstrations against General Noriega that erupted here in the summer of 1987," the *New York Times* observes, while reporting without comment that Col. Hassan, "a favorite of the American and diplomatic establishment here," is to be placed in command of the military with their new 'human rights' orientation after the liberation of Panama by the United States; the ability to tolerate cognitive dissonance is a wondrous trait and a prerequisite to success in the ideological professions. A program of economic warfare was designed to erode Noriega's support among the poor and black population who were his natural constituency, while minimizing the impact on the U.S. business community, a General Accounting Office (GAO) official testified before Congress.[16]

15. Julia Preston, *WP Weekly*, December 25, 1989; AP, December 20; BG, December 21, 1989. On the 1984 elections, see, among other sources, Seymour Hersh, NYT, June 22, 1986; John Weeks, 'Panama: The Roots of Current Political Instability,' *Third World Quarterly*, July 1987; Alfonso Chardy, *Miami Herald*, March 3, 1988; Ken Silverstein, *Columbia Journalism Review*, May/June 1988.
16. Larry Rohter, NYT, January 2, 1990; Paul Blustein and Steven Mufson, *WP Weekly*, December 25, 1989.

One black mark against Noriega was his support for the Contadora peace process for Central America to which the United States was strongly opposed, as usual preferring the arena of violence, in which it reigns supreme, to that of diplomacy, where it is much weaker. His commitment to the war against Nicaragua was in question, and when the Iran-contra affair broke, his usefulness was plainly at an end. A more general problem was his nationalist and populist gestures, a carry-over from the Torrijos period when the traditional white oligarchy was displaced. On New Year's Day 1990, administration of the Panama Canal was to pass largely into Panamanian hands, and a few years later the rest follows. A major oil pipeline is 60 percent owned by Panama. Clearly, traditional U.S. clients had to be restored to power, and there was not much time to spare.

Further gains from the invasion were to tighten the stranglehold around Nicaragua and Cuba which, the government and media complained, had been making use of the free and open Panamanian economy to evade the U.S. trade sanctions and embargo (declared illegal by the World Court, but no matter). These intentions were signalled symbolically by the contemptuous violations of diplomatic immunity, including the break-in at the Nicaraguan Embassy ('by error,' for those who believe in Santa Claus) and repeated detention of Cuban Embassy personnel—all grossly illegal, but that arouses no concern at home apart from the fear of a precedent from which the U.S. might suffer. And there were domestic political gains, as already discussed. Even the vulgar display outside the Vatican Embassy, with rock music blaring and other childish antics, was generally considered good clean fun—and by the military, an imaginative exercise in psychological warfare. The press adhered to the canons of its fabled objectivity, for example, when TV crews in a hotel overlooking the Vatican Embassy displayed a pineapple cut in half outside their room, or when National Public Radio amused its elite intellectual audience with an interview with a fruit and vegetable dealer who was asked whether Noriega's pockmarked face really did look like a pineapple.[17]

All in all, a very successful operation. The United States can now proceed to foster democracy and successful economic development, as it has done with such success in the Caribbean and Central American region for many years. The prospect is seriously put forth, as if history, and the obvious reasons for its regular course, did not exist, another testimony to the stability of the reigning intellectual culture and its remarkable capacity to tolerate absurdity as long as it is serviceable.

Let's finally turn to the general background against which U.S. foreign policy towards Central America will evolve. There are, of course, significant changes underway in the world order. In 1992, Europe will take another step towards integration into a German-dominated confederation. The Soviet Union has not only relaxed its grip over its satellites, but is actually encouraging steps towards freedom and democracy. The rapid collapse of the fragile tyrannies that had been installed by the Soviet army, virtually without bloodshed in most cases, is a remarkable event lacking any close historical precedent.

The Soviet Union has received faint praise in the United States for its restraint. There is little thought, however, that the United States should reciprocate or encourage its satellites to do so. On the contrary, as already discussed, the reaction is to exploit the decline of the Soviet deterrent and to resort more freely to the use of force and other forms of intervention and subversion to bar the way to independent nationalism and desperately needed social change within the traditional U.S. domains. Front-page headlines report Soviet apologies for their invasion of Afghanistan and Czechoslovakia, while commentators sagely discuss the possibility that, finally, the Russians may join the commu-

17. Diego Ribadeneira, BG, December 30, 1989, National Public Radio, reported by Blase Bonpane.

...he United States is also concerned with
...aintaining its dominance over the world's
...ajor energy resources in the Middle East,
...he reason why it continues to bar the way to
...diplomatic settlement of the Arab-Israeli
...onflict.

nity of civilized nations. It is hardly likely that the United States might apologize for the invasion of South Vietnam and the Dominican Republic, the devastation of Cambodia and Laos, the overthrow of the democratic governments of Guatemala and Chile, the dedicated support for near-genocide in Timor, a campaign of international terrorism against Cuba that has no precedent or analogue, a decade of murderous destruction in Central America, and numerous other crimes. In fact, it would take a diligent search to find a voice calling on the United States or its European allies to rise to the moral level of the Kremlin in this regard.

As noted, Soviet military expenditures began to level off in the mid-1970s, and are declining in the course of Gorbachev's attempts to rescue the stagnant command economy. While the militancy of the Reagan administration may have slowed these developments, they did not stop them, and by the mid-1980s Washington was compelled to reduce its aggressiveness, hysterical rhetoric, and military growth as the costs of Reaganite economic mismanagement became unacceptable. Fortuitously, both superpowers, for independent reasons, are on a path away from confrontation.

The dramatic changes in Eastern and Central Europe are a further and quite significant step in the erosion of the bipolar system that emerged from World War II—though it is worthwhile to stress again that the United States was always by far the dominant power and its Soviet rival, a distant second. It has been evident at least since the late stages of the Indochina wars that a new global order has been taking shape, with three major blocs: U.S.-based, Japan-based and a German-based European system. Europe is reconstructing traditional quasi-colonial relations with the East, and Japan is beginning to follow suit. If the United States lags in exploiting this entry into the Western-dominated Third World, it would be left a second class power, an island off the coast of Eurasia. Not surprisingly, the prospect arouses concern.

Though the reasons have changed over the years, the United States has always had a certain ambivalence about the unification of Europe. In the circumstances of the postwar world, it was feared that the Russians had the advantage in the political 'game,' as it was called, so that the game had to be cancelled, with West Germany "walled off from Soviet influence," in George Kennan's phrase.[18] Meanwhile labor and other popular forces were to be undermined and the traditional order largely restored, as elsewhere. The British Foreign Office favored the partition of Germany to bar Soviet influences, viewing "economic and ideological infiltration" from the East as "something very like aggression." Eisenhower too regarded "Soviet political aggression" as the real danger, and saw NATO as a barrier against this threat.

Stalin's 1952 proposal to unify Germany with free elections was flatly rejected because of the condition that a reunited Germany not join a hostile U.S.-run military alliance, a *sine qua non* for any Soviet leadership. Had this and later initiatives been pursued, there might have been no Berlin wall and no invasions of East Berlin, Budapest and Prague.

In the early postwar period, the United States gave substantial support to integration of Western Europe, on the plausible assumption, largely fulfilled, that U.S.-based corporations would gain rich opportunities for investment and profit. As European recovery proceeded, the prospects became less favorable. Currently, the United States looks askance on moves towards European integration that might strengthen its major rivals on the world scene while undermining the U.S. influence that results from East-West

18. For sources, here and below, see my 'Democracy in the Industrial Societies,' Z *Magazine*, January 1988, translated, with sources, in *Linea d'Ombra* (Milan, April 1990); also available in unpublished English ms.

confrontation and the pact system. Its spokesmen call for retaining the NATO and Warsaw Pacts to enhance 'stability'—meaning U.S. influence. European elites have a mixed reaction: exploitation of the East is a tempting prize, but they have their own reasons to be concerned about the loss of a powerful device of population control.

The United States has been undertaking a defensive reaction to the rise of its German- and Japan-based competitors. Since the latter days of the Indochina war, U.S. elites have undertaken intensive efforts to increase corporate profits, weaken unions and the welfare system, temper the 'crisis of democracy' by restoring public apathy, and strengthen state-corporate linkages. They have also sought to solidify the U.S.-controlled bloc. The recent free trade agreement with Canada draws it more closely within the U.S. sphere, and a similar relation with Mexico is not unlikely. The ineffectual Caribbean Basin Initiative was an attempt, which may be revived, to incorporate that region still more tightly within the U.S.-dominated bloc, along with such parts of Latin America as may be economically viable. The United States is also concerned with maintaining its dominance over the world's major energy resources in the Middle East, one reason why it continues to bar the way to a diplomatic settlement of the Arab-Israeli conflict, a matter too complex to pursue here. These efforts are likely to have only limited success, with Japan and Europe increasingly pursuing their own conflicting interests.

With regard to Central America, the U.S. need to control it and repress freedom and democracy there is, if anything, increasing. The capacity to achieve these ends is growing in one respect: the withdrawal of Soviet support for targets of U.S. attack in accord with Gorbachev's 'New Thinking' gives the United States more latitude to impose its will by force and other means, as Elliot Abrams and others rightly conclude.

But the capacity to achieve the traditional ends is declining in other respects. The crucial factor is that indigenous popular forces that are the targets of subversion and violence continue to resist, with remarkable courage and tenacity. A second factor, already noted, is the diversification in the global system, as Europe and Japan pursue their own independent paths. From the point of view of the people of the Third World, this prospect offers some advantages: it is better to have three robbers with their hands in your pocket than only one. Their squabbles over the loot may offer some room for maneuvre, and European solidarity movements might, in principle, play a larger part by influencing their governments and through their own efforts. Domestic dissidence is not a factor to be lightly ignored. Within the United States, though largely outside of established structures, it was strong enough to drive the government underground to clandestine terror instead of the more efficient use of overt force through the 1980s, and continues to impose limits on the exercise of direct violence and other means of coercion, thus to allow some scope for the unending struggle for freedom and justice.

Edinburgh, January 10, 1990

The Tiananmen Square massacre was a bit of a problem. The United States had no objection to it in principle.

Questions and Answers

*Could you give an idea of the long-term aim of all this
benevolence, because it looks like the Japanese are getting
a greater market share?*

Japanese investment in Mexico has been increasing very
fast. There's a degree of intervention in Central America,
and quite a lot in South America (in fact in Brazil, there's a
big Japanese community). To give an indication of the
relative weakness of the United States over the years, Japan
is involved now in actually two exploratory efforts to seek an
alternative to the Panama Canal in Nicaragua—one a
government initiative, one a corporate conglomerate. Now
that's the kind of thing a couple of decades ago that no one
would even mention, before the United States would drive
them out. It would have been completely unacceptable. But
at this point, the United States can't do much about it. So
little, in fact, that these Japanese initiatives are not even
discussed in the United States; I don't think they've even
been reported. So yeah, Japan will try to get in there, and
so will Europe.

Parts of this region, South America in particular, are
traditional European areas of influence and control, for
Britain in particular. During World War II the United States
had to use the weakness of Britain under attack as a way of
driving them out of their traditional Latin American markets. That was one of the reasons why if you look at the
Lend-Lease Bill, you discover that there were conditions in
it saying that Lend-Lease aid could not go to England if
British reserves went above a certain level. Part of the
reason for that was so that the United States could take over

traditional British markets in Latin America. And in some
of these documents where they talk about after the war, and
the need to take over the Latin American military, it's more
pointed than that. What they say is we have to displace the
British and the French from their control of the Latin
American military, so that we can take control of it. And,
undoubtedly, Europe will try to get back into the act, as it
gets stronger, more confident and more willing to confront
the United States. These are the kinds of problems that in
past years led to global wars.

They are not going to do it this time for a number of
reasons. One of them just being the inter-penetration of
capital; the other being exactly what stopped wars in
Europe in 1945. I mean, the history of Europe is a history
of mindless savagery and barbarism, and it terminated in
1945, because the next step would have been the end. And
the same is true of global war. It's a pretty safe prediction,
because if you're wrong, nobody's going to know about it.

*Can I ask you about President Nixon's overtures to the
Chinese?*

Well, it wasn't President Nixon, it was the whole American business community, and the American government.
The Tiananmen Square massacre was a bit of a problem.
The United States had no objection to it in principle. I mean,
the Tiananmen Square massacre, for example, was not
worse than the Kwaugju massacre in 1980 in South Korea.
Probably fewer people were killed than in the Kwaugju
massacre, which was extremely barbaric, and in fact Korea
used troops that had been under American command, and
nobody cared. It was barely reported; President Carter, (who
was president at the time) made some statements about
how South Korea isn't ready yet for democracy and that sort
of thing. Tiananmen Square was pretty horrible, but it was
the same kind of thing. Basically nobody cared.

There was a problem with Tiananmen Square. The

problem was that the press was all over the place. Gorbachev had just been there; the whole international press corps was there, television cameras were focusing on it, and it was just a stupid mistake to carry out a massacre under a glare of television lights. That's not the way you do it. You wait until people are looking the other way.

Furthermore, there's a kind of contradiction in the way the United States deals with China. On the one hand it's a reflex in the press, that when an 'official enemy' carries out some atrocity you go berserk, because of your deep feelings for human rights—which are somehow suppressed when 'our side' is responsible for similar, or worse, atrocities. On the other hand, China's an ally. It's been an ally since the 1970s. So it's kind of an enemy, because it's an official communist power; but it's also an ally. You're kind of stuck. So they reported the Tiananmen Square massacre, and everyone shed the proper tears, but it was well understood that this was for show, and for what propaganda gains that could be had from it. Shortly after the massacre, *Business Week*, which is the expression of liberal business opinion, was saying, "Look, we can't let this get out of hand, because the commercial interests in China are too important, and we have to re-establish them."

We now know that it's been admitted that within a month after the massacre, National Security Adviser Brent Scowcroft was sent to China (the official story was that he was sent to China to tell them about our deep feelings for human rights, but the actual story will come out in 30 years, when the documents are released)—to assure the Chinese leaders that we don't mean any of this stuff. In fact, just a couple of days after the Tiananmen Square massacre, George Bush's brother went to China to firm up a contract that he had arranged in Shanghai, for a golf course or something like that. It was clear—you've got to put this in perspective—China's an important ally and good business partner. When the government announced they were selling $300 million worth of communications and other high tech equipment to China, the White House spokesman said, "Look, this is $300 million worth of business for American firms." It's kind of interesting...some commentators in the United States noticed that there was something funny about invading Panama to save human rights while we on the same day announce that we're sending $300 million worth of high tech equipment to China, to leaders whose human rights record was a thousand times worse. So a couple of people said, "Gee, this seems kind of inconsistent, what's going on?" Nobody would point out the obvious— that it's not the least bit inconsistent, it's completely consistent. In both cases it's good for business, and that's the consistent feature. It's not Nixon.

Nixon, whatever you think about him, is a kind of statesman. He has a grasp of world affairs, and says what he thinks—he makes some sense. But, the same thinking was going on on the part of everyone else. China was an important market, and place for cheap labor, where you can pay much less and get them to work much harder than you can in Hong Kong these days.

What's the American role in the Iran-Iraq war?

We can only speculate about that because there's no real documentary record, but it looks as though the U.S. role was to keep it going, as it was for most of the world—the Soviet Union, Western Europe, etc. The best thing was to have them kill each other, because both Iraq and Iran were problems. They were both nationalist regimes with independent interests (brutal and so on but nobody much cares about that). They were a nationalist threat, and they could have been a spreading threat. So as long as they're killing each other, it's not too much of a problem.

So, the idea was to supply both sides, as the United States and its allies in fact supplied both sides. Now, towards the end, Iran's preponderant power was beginning to show, and it looked as if they were going to win, and that's no good. So the United States intervened to prevent that, and to support Iraq. So, the move to send American warships into the Gulf which was called 'freedom of shipping' or something—that was actually to block Iran. Freedom of shipping in the Gulf was actually threatened by Iraq, not by Iran, for a very simple reason. Iraq had pipelines for its oil, and Iran didn't. In fact, even when an American ship was attacked by Iraqi forces, they still went after Iran, because the idea was to shift the balance so that it would be a standoff. Since then the United States has been rebuilding its relations with Iraq—they've just announced again, right in the middle of the Panama invasion, that they're relaxing loan sanctions—and they're trying to restore connections with Iran, too, to bring them into the American sphere.

Do you see any optimism in the future that the U.S. domestic population might be able to exert more influence on the administration in these global aspirations, given the fact that the perception of the 'evil enemy' Russia has dissipated somewhat?

Well, that's going to be interesting to see. Panama is the first real test when it was necessary to invade another country without the pretext of the Russians, and it worked neatly. How long you can go along with that I don't know. The Russians were a very convincing threat—they're violent, they've got missiles, they're brutal, they do all sorts of horrible things, and they're big and powerful and so on—that's a real threat. People like Quaddaffi and Noriega, you can turn them into short-term threats, but it's pretty hard to carry off for a long period.

I think the same's true for the 'war on drugs.' You can get people terrified of narco-traffickers, but how long is it going to be before they see that the problem is not in Colombia and in the slums, the problem is 'social policy' basically. If you're worried about substance abuse, you can't only be concerned with the maybe 5,000 deaths a year from illicit drugs, also you're going to be concerned with the 300,000 deaths a year from tobacco, 200,000 deaths a year from alcohol...so many questions have got to be asked. The United States, incidentally, is one of the major narco-traffickers in the world, forcing Asian countries to take tobacco under the threat of trade sanctions. I don't suspect the anti-drug hysteria will last long. It's going to be interesting to see what kind of threat can be conjured up to keep the domestic population under control.

I wouldn't assume that it can't be done. There's 80 years of experience on the part of a very sophisticated public relations industry, and a very well disciplined intellectual class that has long been committed to this. And there are a lot of things you can think of that might work, but it's not going to be as simple as one might think.

I'd like your comments on American policy in relation to the Palestinian problem.

Well, the Palestinians are one of the nationalist forces that are just in the way and since 1967—shortly after the '67 war—the United States has been very impressed with Israel's capacity to use force. That's always impressed them. When Israel won the war so handily in '67, U.S. support for Israel shot way up. Since then, Israel's been what's regarded as a strategic asset.

This is not particularly new. We now know that as far back as 1948, with Britain withdrawing from the region, the Joint Chiefs of Staff identified Israel as a strategic asset, as a base for the exercise of American power in the region. Through the 1950s that increased; in 1967 the alliance was set. But to keep Israel as a strategic asset, [meaning a base for the use—or at least threat—of American power in the region, to keep down independent nationalism, and also as a (by now) mercenary state that can be called upon to carry out ugly actions around the world, (for example, providing arms to Noriega—when the United States was still support-ing him.)], to keep that relationship going, you really have to keep Israel embattled.

A political settlement would take the lid off, as it would elsewhere—it would mean Israel would become integrated into the region, domestic regional politics would begin to develop, etc. The United States has been opposed to settlement there since about 1970, and it's the main barrier to a political settlement. There could possibly be at least a political settlement to the Arab-Israeli conflict and the whole world knows what it is. There's enormous interna-tional consensus behind one or another variety of 'two-state' settlement. It's been feasible, certainly since the mid-70s, when the United States first vetoed it at the U.N. when it was introduced by the Arab states and the PLO, and it remains feasible, but it won't happen because the United States will block it.

In fact, it's kind of intriguing to watch the way the press in the United States deals with this issue. The *New York Times* has conceded in fact—there's a line that you can find somewhere embedded in a story—that the United States is the only country in the world that is supporting what is called the 'Shamir plan' (which is actually the 'Baker-Peres-Shamir plan'). That's a plan which bars the possibility of any political settlement. Its basic premise is that there can be no additional Palestinian state (meaning in addition to Jordan — already considered a 'Palestinian' state), and there can be no change in the status of Judea, Sumeria and Gaza, except according to the guidelines of the Israeli government, which rules out any Palestinian self-determination—that's the 'Peres-Shamir-Baker plan.'

...the United States has been rebuilding i

relations with Iraq—they've just announce

again, right in the middle of the Panam

invasion, that they're relaxing loan sanction

Noam Chomsky:
A Select Bibliography

•*Political Economy of Human Rights* (with Edward Herman) Vol 1: *The Washington Connection and Third World Fascism;* Vol 2: *After the Cataclysm—Post-war Indochina and the Reconstruction of Imperial Ideology,* Black Rose (Canada)/South End (US),1979

•*Radical Priorities,* Black Rose (Canada), 1982

•*Cartesian Linguistics: A Chapter in the History of Rationalist Thought,* University Press of America (US), 1983

•*Fateful Triangle: Israel, the United States and the Palestinians,* Black Rose (Canada)/South End (US),1984

•*Logical Structure of Linguistic Theory,* University of Chicago Press (US), 1985

•*Turning the Tide: United States Intervention in Central America and the Struggle for Peace,* Black Rose (Canada)/South End (US), 1986

•*Knowledge of Language: Its Nature, Origins and Use,* Praeger (US), 1986

•*Pirates and Emperors: International Terrorism in the Real World,* Black Rose (Canada)/Amana (US), 1987

•*Language and Problems of Knowledge: The Managua Lectures,* MIT Press (US), 1987

•*The Chomsky Reader,* Serpent's Tail (UK)/Pantheon (US), 1988

•*The Culture of Terrorism,* Black Rose (Canada)/South End (US), 1988.

•*On Power and Ideology: Managua Lectures,* Black Rose (Canada)/South End (US), 1988

•*Language and Politics,* Black Rose (Canada), 1988

•*Chomsky Reader,* Serpents Tail (UK)/Pantheon (US), 1988

•*Manufacturing Consent: the Politcial Economy of Mass Media* (with Edward Herman), Pantheon (US), 1988

•*Necessary Illusions: Thought Control in Democratic Societies* (with Edward Herman), Pluto Press (UK)/South End (US), 1989

•Also a regular contributor to Z Magazine, published by the Institute for Social and Cultural Change, (US)

These are available mail order from AK Press. Write for catalog.